Montauk

Montauk Point Lighthouse at Christmas

A Local's Guide to Montauk, New York in 2 Days - From the Ocean to the Hills

By Vanessa Gordon

Table of Contents

Introduction...5
Day 1...7
   7:30 am -- Breakfast at Mary's Marvelous......................7
   8:15 am -- The Walking Dunes Trail - Hither Hills State Park..9
   10:15 am -- Shopping at Gosman's Dock........................11
   11:45 am -- Tour of the Montauk Point Lighthouse....13
   1:40 pm -- Lunch at Navy Beach..16
   3:15 pm -- Explore the Montauk Village.........................19
   5:15 pm -- Massage or Spa Treatment at Gurney's......20
   7:15 pm -- Dinner at Indian Wells Tavern......................22
   9:00 pm -- Music at The Stephen Talkhouse.................24
Day 2...25
   8:15 am -- Breakfast Goldberg's Famous Bagels..........25
   9:10 am -- Rita's Stables - Beach Horseback Riding....27
   11:30 am -- Puff n' Putt Family Fun Center...................29
   12:40 pm -- Lunch - The Clam Bar....................................31
   2:15 pm -- Dessert at The Candied Anchor...................34
   3:00 pm -- Second House Museum.................................35
   4:15 pm -- Theodore Roosevelt State Park (aka Montauk County Park)..37
   6:15 pm -- Dinner at Zum Schneider...............................39
Things You Need to Know..41
   Before you go..41
   Transportation tips...42
   Communications..43
   Parking..43
   Restaurants..43
   Climate..50
   Hotels..50
   Money - ATMs, credit cards & the currency..................51
   Getting into Montauk...51
   Nightlife..51

Additional websites for information 52
Random tips 52
ABOUT THE AUTHOR 55
UNANCHOR WANTS YOUR OPINION! 57
OTHER UNANCHOR ITINERARIES 58

Introduction

If you are looking for a seaside town rich in history, a double dose of relaxation, a family friendly hamlet, and a little spice of adventure, search no further then Montauk, New York. The sky is truly the limit for your vacation to the very tip of the eastern end of Long Island.

Recently declared by *Paris Vogue* as the "new St. Tropez," Montauk is a favorite location for those that are looking for a relaxing getaway that has so much more to offer then just lounging by the beach with cocktails. Although Montauk certainly does have some of the most beautiful beaches in the world, mixed with a low-key surfing town, it is a vibrant, friendly community that will have you coming back for many years to come.

Montauk, and the neighboring town of Amagansett, are lovely to visit in the spring and autumn as well as the summer, being its busiest time of year. This itinerary will highlight not only what the best of Montauk has to offer, but when and where to seek the best deals, spas, happy hours, and more from an individual who has lived near and worked in Montauk for over a decade.

Vanessa Gordon

Day 1

============

7:30 am -- Breakfast at Mary's Marvelous

- **Price:** $25.00 (for a single adult)
- **Duration:** 30 minutes
- **Address:** 207 Main St, Amagansett, NY 11930 (631) 267-8796

This is one of my favorite places in Amagansett (and in nearby East Hampton, where they have a separate location) to grab a bite to eat. You must try their freshly brewed coffee, cold pressed watermelon juice, and one of their freshly baked scones. Grab some "Mary-O's" to bring home.

There is a small round table in the front near the window and plenty of benches on Main Street and across the way in the shopping commons. Just note that this quaint little nook does become crowded between 9am and 10am in the morning and again between 12pm and 1:30pm in the afternoon.

Please read my review for Mary's Marvelous at: http://eastendtaste.com/lunch-break-at-marys-marvelous/

*Cost is approximate for 2 people.

Drive to Hither Hills State Park
tion: 15 minutes

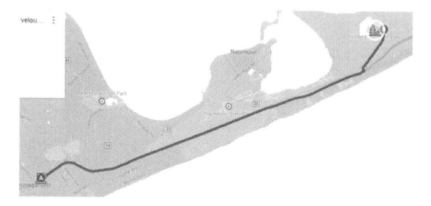

Here's the link to my map: goo.gl/uYoY2P

Taxis are available and it is also a pleasant biking trip. However, to be quite honest, it is unfortunate to say that there really are no "top notch" taxi services in the Hamptons due to their high prices and inconsistent performance. If I were to choose one company it would be, Lindy's: 631-907-1111.

Head east on Montauk Highway for about five miles through the Napeague stretch. You will first pass the Clam Bar and then Cyril's Fish House on your left. Just before the right hand exit onto Old Montauk Highway, make a left onto Hwy to Napeague. The destination and parking will be on your left.

8:15 am -- The Walking Dunes Trail - Hither Hills State Park

- **Price:** $10.00 (for a single adult)
- **Duration:** 1 hour and 45 minutes
- **Address:** 164 Old Montauk Hwy, Montauk, NY 11954 (631) 668-2554

A 3/4-mile trail that loops through one of the worlds most fascinating dune areas. Some of the dunes reach as high as 80 feet tall. This park also offers fishing year round, biking, and cross-country skiing. Hither Hills also has 168 campsites along with hiking and nature trails. There are 18 different trails that cover 40 miles of terrain. I highly recommend purchasing a map in town or asking for one at your resort.

The park is open year round from sunrise to sunset. The $10 cost is the parking fee if you are not camping. Parking is at either the overlook at Hither Woods (where the directions take you) or at the Eddie Ecker County Park parking lot (200 Navy St).

10:00 am -- Drive to Gosman's Dock

- **Duration:** 15 minutes

Continue heading east on Montauk Highway and continue toward the large roundabout in the center of town (about 4.8 miles). Make a left onto The Plaza and then turn left onto S Edgemere St. Continue onto Flamingo Ave. You will pass the Montauk train station on your right. Go straight at the four-way intersection, the road will turn into County Rd 77. Turn right onto West Lake Dr where you will reach the parking area for Gosman's Dock.

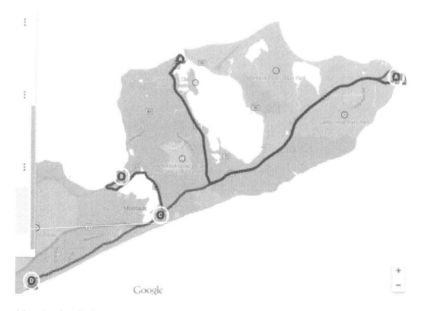

Here's the link to my map: goo.gl/xdCPtT

10:15 am -- Shopping at Gosman's Dock

- **Price:** $150.00 (for a single adult)
- **Duration:** 1 hour and 15 minutes
- **Address:** 500 W Lake Dr Montauk, NY 11954

If this is your first or even fifth time visiting Montauk, a trip to Gosman's Dock is a mandatory stop. There are a few unique shops that sell gorgeous jewelry, pillows, nautical themed place settings and dishes, fresh, local seafood, a Ben and Jerry's, and a perfect view of the fishing and recreational boats going in and out of the harbor.

If you are feeling peckish, head over to **Gosman's Clam Bar** that offers affordable family fare such as whole lobsters, lobster rolls, combo plates, fried seafood, grilled fish, along with side orders of corn on the cob, and coleslaw. Order at the counter and eat at their outside patio under the umbrellas overlooking the Harbor where you get a bird's eye view of the fishing boats coming in and out. Watch your food carefully as the seagulls show no mercy. On occasion, I have seen seagulls snatch whole lobster rolls!

- Drive to the Montauk Point Lighthouse

- **Duration:** 15 minutes

When you exit Gosman's Dock, turn left onto W Lake Dr. Stay on W Lake Dr. for ten minutes until you reach Montauk Highway. Make a left onto Montauk Highway all the way to the end. You will see the lighthouse on your right hand side. Parking is just opposite the lighthouse, the entrance is just opposite the gift shop.

11:45 am -- Tour of the Montauk Point Lighthouse

- **Price:** FREE
- **Duration:** 1 hour and 30 minutes
- **Address:** 2000 New York 27, Montauk, NY 11954 (631) 668-2544

No trip to Montauk is complete without a tour of the Montauk Point Lighthouse. I still come to the lighthouse at least once a year to take photos of where the ocean and the cliffs meet.

If you visit during the holidays, they have a Christmas lighting event usually held on the first weekend of December. The lighthouse lighting is during an evening on a Saturday and a family-friendly event with pony rides, Santa Claus, and more happens the following Sunday during the day.

Below are photos of a trip to the lighthouse I took during the holidays, the first is from the lookout point and the last is an interior shot:

1:15 pm -- Drive to Navy Beach

- **Duration:** 25 minutes

Follow Montauk Highway all the way to the Montauk Village until you reach The Plaza (the circle). Make the first right onto S Edgemere St. Pass the Surf Lodge on your left, and then take the next left onto Industrial Rd. At the next main intersection, make a slight right onto 2nd House Rd. Just before the end of the road (the road may be a bit bumpy), turn right onto Navy Rd. The restaurant will be on your left.

*Make sure you park in the restaurant parking lots rather than the residential parking.

1:40 pm -- Lunch at Navy Beach

- **Price:** $90.00 (for a single adult)
- **Duration:** 1 hour and 20 minutes
- **Address:** 16 Navy Rd, Montauk, NY 11954 (631) 668-6868

The seaside views at this restaurant are breathtaking. This family-friendly restaurant serves American comfort cuisine, in a laid back beachfront. Most of these dishes feature local seafood from Gosman's Dock and produce from east end farms. Inside, you will find a traditional, nautical theme that will transport you back in time to when this beach was occupied by the US Navy, hence the name.

My favorite dishes for lunch are their Yunnan Ribs appetizer, the Jumbo Lump Crab Cake, the Buttermilk Fried Chicken (I LOVE their spicy honey drizzle, be sure to ask for extra), and the Navy Burger with their famous Bacon-Onion Marmalade. For dessert, you must try the Peanut Butter Cake.

Please read my detailed review of the restaurant : www.eastendtaste.com/navy-beach-for-lunch

*Cost is approximate for 2 people.

3:00 pm -- Drive to Montauk Village

- **Duration:** 15 minutes

Make a right out of Navy Beach onto Navy Rd. Make a left onto 2nd House Rd. In 0.7 miles, make a slight left onto Industrial Rd. Continue for just under a mile on Industrial Rd and then turn right onto Edgmere St. Turn right onto The Plaza then make an immediate right turn onto Montauk Highway.

Local's tip: *The best parking is just near Chase Bank.*

3:15 pm -- Explore the Montauk Village

- **Price:** $150.00 (for a single adult)
- **Duration:** 1 hour and 45 minutes
- **Address:** 731 Montauk Hwy Montauk, NY 11954

Montauk Village offers a spectacular shopping experience. In town, explore surf shops, a natural food shop, a nostalgic toy and game shop, a fudge shop on (**Fudge N Stuff** on South Edgemere St), a book shop, plenty of surf shops, boutiques that sell fashionable beachwear, and so much more. **Vintage Pink** on Montauk Highway is a cute little shop, **Kai Kai Sandals** on Main St for apparel, and you must stop in to **Landshark** for gifts and Montauk apparel for everyone in your family.

5:00 pm -- Drive to Gurney's Resort and Spa

- **Duration:** 15 minutes

Head west on Montauk Highway and turn left onto Old Montauk Highway. Continue for just over two miles, Gurney's Inn will be on your left. Valet parking is available.

5:15 pm -- Massage or Spa Treatment at Gurney's

- **Price:** $150.00 (for a single adult)
- **Duration:** 1 hour and 45 minutes
- **Address:** 290 Old Montauk Hwy Montauk, NY 11954 (631) 668-2345

You must take a swim in their seawater pool. It is the most soothing experience and really helps to relax your muscles. Offered to you are numerous organic signature body treatments and therapies including seaweed wraps, organic facials, manicures, pedicures, and more. Check out the resort for events happening throughout the year including their Spatini event in July, fitness retreats (and classes), and weekend events.

If you are not staying at Gurney's, there is a $40 fee per person to use the facilities, including the fitness center, the seawater pool, and the spa. The seawater spa is open seven days a week. Please call to make an appointment.

Website: http://www.gurneysmontauk.com

*Cost is approximate per person and includes one standard massage and the facility fee.

7:00 pm -- Drive to Indian Wells Tavern

- **Duration:** 15 minutes

Turn left out of Gurney's Inn. Continue on Old Montauk Highway until you reach the entrance to Montauk Highway. Continue on Montauk Hwy through the Napeague stretch and into the town of Amagansett, passing the Shell gas station and the firehouse on your right. You will drive for a total of seven miles on Montauk Hwy. The restaurant will be on your right just past Mary's Marvelous and across the street from Amagansett Square.

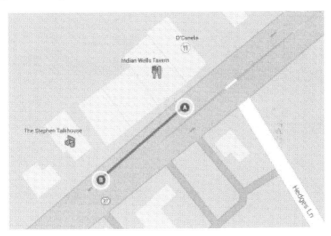

Here's the link to my map: goo.gl/TbJzj4

⁓m -- Dinner at Indian Wells Ṯavern

- **Price:** $120.00 (for a single adult)
- **Duration:** 1 hour and 30 minutes
- **Address:** 177 Main St, Amagansett, NY 11930 (631) 267-0400

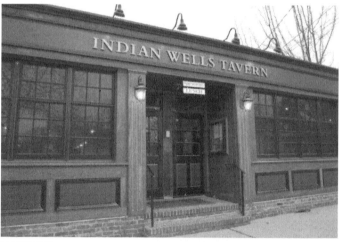

This is an awesome, casual restaurant located in the heart of Amagansett Village. Open year round, the restaurant serves up American fare with a friendly hometown pub atmosphere. There is a spacious bar with widescreen televisions and they offer daily specials.

My favorite dishes on their menu include their Arugula salad ($12), crispy Mahi Mahi fish tacos ($19), turkey burger with a cranberry aioli ($13), and the banana taco for dessert ($8).

This is a very popular restaurant so I do recommend calling ahead for availability. For more information, visit their website at http://www.indianwellstavern.com.

Please note: *This restaurant is NOT stroller friendly or wheelchair accessible. An option instead for dinner could be* **LUNCH** *(Lobster Roll) that is both stroller friendly and wheelchair accessible.*

*Cost is approximate for 2 people.

8:45 pm -- Walk to the Stephen Talkhouse

- **Duration:** 15 minutes

Make a right when exiting Indian Wells Tavern. The Stephen Talkhouse is just a few businesses down on your right.

-- Music at The Stephen ...use

- **Price:** $50.00 (for a single adult)
- **Duration:** 2 hours and 30 minutes
- **Address:** 161 Main St Amagansett, NY 11930 (631) 267-3117

The Stephen Talkhouse has been in operation since the mid 1980's. This is a very popular and lively place to hang out into the wee hours of the night. Phenomenal bands and solo musicians play here on a regular basis. The bartenders are extremely congenial and the entire place is very down-to-earth with its low ceilings and wooden bar. Do check their calendar for events on their website: http://stephentalkhouse.com

Please note: *To enter, you must be 21 or over with an ID. There is usually a coverage charge between $10-20 per person.*

*Cost is approximate for two people, including a $10 cover charge per person.

Day 2

8:15 am -- Breakfast Goldberg's Famous Bagels

- **Price:** $25.00 (for a single adult)
- **Duration:** 45 minutes
- **Address:** 28 S Etna Ave, Montauk, NY 11954 (631) 238-5977

Goldberg's Famous Bagels, a local hotspot and favorite, is a deli and bakery that has several stores throughout the east end, including Napeague, East Hampton, and Southampton. In addition to their famous bagels and flagels (a flat bagel), breakfast menu items include sandwiches, eggs, omelettes, and French toast.

This is also a great place to stop at for a quick lunch. This location is open at 6am and closes at 4pm.

*Cost is approximate for 2 people.

9:00 am -- Drive to Rita's Stable

- **Duration:** 10 minutes

Rita's Stable is located one mile east of Montauk village. Make a right onto S Etna Ave, or head northeast towards S Essex St. Turn left onto S Essex St and take the first right turn onto Montauk Highway. Continue for just under a mile (you will see Shadmoor State Park on your right during most your drive), then turn left onto West Lake Drive, stable driveway will be on your right.

9:10 am -- Rita's Stables - Beach Horseback Riding

- **Price:** $150.00 (for a single adult)
- **Duration:** 2 hours and 5 minutes
- **Address:** 3 West Lake Drive Montauk, NY 11954 (631) 668-5453

At this super friendly stable, experience horseback riding on pristine trails and on the beaches in small groups. Catch some breathtaking views along scenic trails. This is a perfect tour if you love horses like I do. The people who own and run the stable are very friendly and helpful and the horses are very well tamed. Private guided rides are also available.

The stable has been apart of the community for over 30 years. Be sure to visit their farm animals that roam freely, including donkeys, sheep, rabbits, chickens, ducks, geese, and peacocks. Photo opportunities are abundant! Pony rides and parties are available as well.

Hours of operation are 9am-6pm and they are open year round. They accept cash, MasterCard, and Visa.

*Cost is approximate for two people.

11:15 am -- Drive to Puff n' Putt

- **Duration:** 15 minutes

Head southeast on W Lake Dr. Make a right onto Montauk Hwy. Continue through the Plaza and Montauk village, or just over a mile. The destination is just after 7-Eleven on your right-hand side.

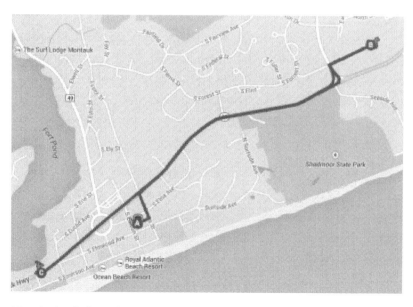

Here's the link to the map: goo.gl/vnPHWl

11:30 am -- Puff n' Putt Family Fun Center

- **Price:** $35.00 (for a single adult)
- **Duration:** 1 hour
- **Address:** 659 Montauk Highway, Montauk, NY. 11954 (631) 668-4473

Take yourself back to your childhood years at this nostalgic mini golf and arcade center. They also offer boat, canoe, and paddleboard rentals, and you may choose to stay here for a few hours or come back later in the afternoon. Plenty of photo opportunities and a chance to score a free game at the last hole. This is a great opportunity to unwind and have some fun before lunch.

*Cost is approximate for 2 people.

***Please note:** *NO credit cards are accepted, cash only!*

12:30 pm -- Drive to The Clam Bar

- **Duration:** 10 minutes

Continue on Montauk Highway, over the hill for about seven minutes or 5.7 miles. The restaurant will be on your right. Ample parking is available in front of the restaurant.

Here's a link to the map: goo.gl/urU6yi

12:40 pm -- Lunch - The Clam Bar

- **Price:** $70.00 (for a single adult)
- **Duration:** 1 hour and 20 minutes
- **Address:** 2025 Montauk Hwy, Amagansett, NY 11930 (631) 267-6348

The Clam Bar offers some of the most delicious seafood on the east end, including my favorite lobster roll ($19.50), clam strips, soups of the day including their seafood corn chowder, and their whole lobster. I love that with their lobster roll they use a potato hot dog roll and the lobster meat is piled high. Everything is so fresh and I love the outdoor seating in the summer. You must order their sweet potato fries as a side! If you are in the mood for dessert, try their sea salt caramel cheesecake. This restaurant is very child-friendly.

Please read my review of the Clam Bar: http://eastendtaste.com/clam-bar-at-napeague-for-lunch/

Note: *CASH only! There is an ATM on site.*

*The cost is approximate for 2 people.

Menu from the Clam Bar

2:00 pm -- Drive to The Candied Anchor

- **Duration:** 15 minutes

Turn left on Montauk Highway, continue on Montauk Highway for 6.2 miles, passing the 7-Eleven on your left and the Memory Motel and Bar on your right. The destination will be just after S Embassy St on your left and is located adjacent to the Montauk Bike Shop.

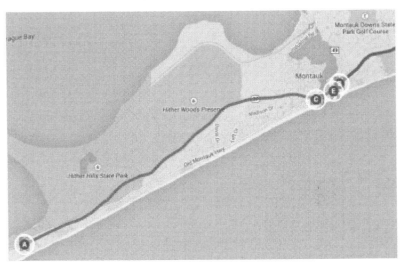

Here's a link to the map: goo.gl/urU6yi

2:15 pm -- Dessert at The Candied Anchor

- **Price:** $18.00 (for a single adult)
- **Duration:** 30 minutes
- **Address:** 721 Montauk Highway, Montauk, NY 11954 (631) 668-8038

This whimsical and colorful candy shop is located in the heart of Montauk and offers old-fashioned candies and locally fresh baked goods. Baked goods include adorable pies in a jar, scrumptious and moist brownies and cookies, and marshmallows. Take some relief from the heat with locally made ice pops and refreshing Sweet'tauk lemonade, a Montauk original. Indulge at this nautically sweet candy shop and send your taste buds on a whirlwind journey. My favorite candies here are the chocolate seashells and caramels. Throwing a party? The Candied Anchor does catering and will create a very special cake for you.

Note: *Closed on Wednesdays*

For more information, please visit http://www.candiedanchor.com

*Cost is approximate for 2 people.

2:45 pm -- Drive to the Second House Museum

- **Duration:** 15 minutes

Make a right onto Montauk Highway, pass S Embassy St., then S Emery St. You will also pass the 7-Eleven and then the Puff n' Putt Family Fun Center on your right. Drive for a total of 0.4 miles. The destination will be on your right.

The museum is located directly across the street from the Oceanside Beach Resort. There will be a green sign that says "Second House Museum / Built in 1797." Pull into their driveway; there is plenty of parking in their back lot.

3:00 pm -- Second House Museum

- **Price:** $10.00 (for a single adult)
- **Duration:** 1 hour
- **Address:** Address is Approximate: 626 Montauk Highway Montauk, NY 11954 (631) 668-5340

This is the oldest and most historic building still standing in Montauk. Built in 1797, during the summer, there are a few Native American events, craft fairs, and events held on their lawn. Their garden is so picturesque during the warm months with plenty of photo opportunities.

$5 admission for adults, $2 for children.

Please note the museum is open from Memorial Day through Columbus Day from 10am to 4pm and is **closed on Wednesday.** An option instead is to visit the famous surfing beach, **Ditch Plains** at 40 Ditch Plains Rd, Montauk or the hiking trails of Shadmoor Park, 900 Montauk Highway, Montauk.

4:00 pm -- Drive to the Theodore Roosevelt State Park (aka Montauk County Park)

- **Duration:** 15 minutes

Make a left and continue east on Montauk Hwy, through the village of Montauk. Pass East Lake Drive and the entrance to Deep Hollow Ranch. The parking side and entrance will be on your left, or the north side of Montauk Hwy.

Total driving distance is approximately three miles.

Here's a link to the map: goo.gl/urU6yi

4:15 pm -- Theodore Roosevelt State Park (aka Montauk County Park)

- **Price:** FREE
- **Duration:** 1 hour and 45 minutes
- **Address:** Address is Approximate: 1640 Montauk Hwy Montauk, NY (631) 852-7878 or 852-7879

This state park, adjacent to the village of Montauk, is rich in history and is one of the best locations to combine a hiking experience with a visit to a beach. You just can't visit Montauk without at least a trip or two to one of the many fabulous beaches.

The hiking trail begins at Third House, a historic landmark, and winds upward through fields, pastures, and up to the summit of a hill where, weather permitting, you are able to have stunning ocean views and even see as far as the coast of New England. Other landmarks within the park include Ogden's Brook, Oyster Pond, and what remains of a Native American settlement. If you want to expand your hike, beyond Theodore Roosevelt County Park is Camp Hero and Montauk Point State Parks.

The Third House played a significant role in 1898 when it was the headquarters for Camp Wikoff. Following their victory in the Spanish-American War, Teddy Roosevelt and the Rough Riders, as well as 28,000 soldiers suffering from contagious diseases, were quarantined at Camp Wikoff. The park was renamed in 1998 as the Theodore Roosevelt State Park as part of the centennial anniversary.

6:00 pm -- Drive to Zum Schneider

- **Price:** FREE
- **Duration:** 15 minutes

Exit the state park and make a right onto Montauk Highway and drive for about 5.2 miles. Pass the Puff n' Putt Family Fun Center and then the 7-Eleven on your right then at the next three-way intersection, make a right onto S Emery St. You will immediately see the restaurant on your left-hand side.

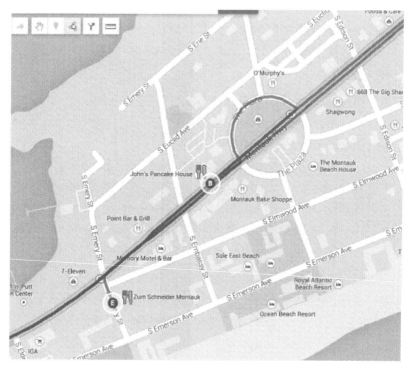

Here's a link to the map: goo.gl/urU6yi

6:15 pm -- Dinner at Zum Schneider

- **Price:** $80.00 (for a single adult)
- **Duration:** 1 hour and 45 minutes
- **Address:** 4 South Elmwood Ave Montauk, NY 11954
  Phone number (631) 238-5963

Zum Schneider serves up delicious Bavarian cuisine and has a wide variety of German beers on tap. Come here if you really want to have a lively and super fun dining experience, meet new friends, and be greeted and served by some of the friendliest staff in the Hamptons. There are plenty of small plates options if you choose to come in for drinks and snacks. My favorite dishes are their Weiner Schnitzel ($23) and the Gebackener Camembert, baked camembert with lingonberry jam, a fresh roll and a house salad for $15.

Note: *The kitchen closes at 11pm and accepts* **CASH only***!*

*Cost is approximate for 2 people.

Storefront of the Zum Schneider

Things You Need to Know

Before you go

Take note of the time of year you decide to visit. For example, the summer season is the busiest time of year in Amagansett and Montauk, with droves of individuals visiting from all over the country. If you wish to visit during the summer, I highly recommend, if you can, visiting on a weekday. Even though the prices are hiked up significantly during the summer months (Memorial Day in late May to Labor Day in early September), you will find better deals during the weekdays. Avoid Memorial Day and Labor Day weekend if you do not wish to mingle in the crowds and heavy traffic. In the summer, make reservations for hotels at least a month in advance. Most people may not know this, but a very fun time to visit Montauk is during the autumn season when there is the Hamptons International Film Festival that stretches from Montauk to Southampton (further west), and when the farmers markets and fairs are still going strong. The autumn season is also a spectacular time to snag gifts and dine out at very reasonable prices.

This is a **seasonal destination**; however, you will always find a number of fun things to do during the winter months. Think cross-country skiing through the trails and holiday celebrations and tree lightings across town and at the famous Montauk Point Lighthouse.

In addition to hotel reservations, book your bus trip ticket at least a week in advance. If you can, avoid traveling on Friday evenings to Montauk and leaving the area on a Sunday afternoon.

Transportation tips

- If you are able to, avoid taking **taxis** at all costs. It is much cheaper to rent a car during your stay. **Enterprise** is located in the Hampton Jitney bus stop in Southampton, NY on Montauk Highway. Taxi trips can cost as much as $40-50 for a one-way, twenty-minute trip.
- **Buses** are your best bet for commuting to the city. The *Hampton Jitney* and *Hamptons Luxury Liner* are the most well known forms of bus transportation. They are consistently on time and professional. New bus services have emerged recently including the *Bolt Bus*. The Hampton Jitney charges $30 one-way, $53 round trip. If you intend to visit the Hamptons in the future, the jitney tickets never expire (ever!) and you may consider purchasing a ten-ticket pack. (www.hamptonjitney.com)
- The cheapest way to visit the Hamptons is via the **LIRR**. The only downside is that there are two stopovers on the train, one in Jamaica, Queens and then one in Ronkonkoma, Long Island. The schedule also has limited times whereas the buses run every hour, to and from the Hamptons. The train station and bus station in East Hampton, for example, let you off in the heart of the village, with easy walking distance to hotels, restaurants, and shops. (new.mta.info/lirr)
- Take advantage of *Hamptons Ride* in Montauk during the summer, offering complimentary transportation from the Oceanside Resort to the Atlantic Terrace on ocean side roads in the Village, stopping to drop and board passengers along the way. You can see the route on their website. (thefreeride.com/hamptons)

Communications

Local radio stations include WLNG, 92.1 FM that provides information on local news, businesses, and events, oldies music, and live programming. Beach 101.7 FM plays top 40; WPPB, 88.3 FM, Peconic Bay Public Broadcasting, offers local news and NPR staples. The areas local papers are *The East Hampton Star*, *Dan's Papers*, *The Independent*, and *The East Hampton Press*.

Parking

Free parking is available on most village streets. Watch for those time limits! Most are one or two hour parking lots/spaces. There are three public parking lots in Montauk's village: one opposite the post office, one on South Elmwood Avenue at Embassy Street, and the last one is located by the Hampton Jitney stop on South Euclid Street. Do not attempt to park in the two-hour or one-hour **parking spaces** AND think you could stay any longer than the allotted time. They are very aggressive with giving parking tickets and it is always very crowded.

Restaurants

Additional restaurants I recommend:

Amagansett/Napeague

- **Zakura**: This is my favorite Japanese restaurant on the outskirts of East Hampton off of Montauk Highway. Their prices are very reasonable and they offer very good sushi. Many locals frequent this restaurant. They

make an excellent leche martini. I love their avocado salad, dumplings (gyoza), and their specialty sushi rolls. For dessert, be sure to try their leche sorbet or their fried cheesecake, depending upon your appetite. Open year round.
- **Hampton Chutney**: This eatery, located in Amagansett Square, serves delicious dosas and chutneys. If you decide to come here, you must try their cold pressed juices and mango lassis. The cardamom coffee here is particularly tasty. Take out orders and outdoor seating. They also have a location in NYC. Open seasonally.

Montauk

The Seawater Grill at Gurney's

This is a terrific restaurant located inside Gurney's Inn Resort and Spa that hosts a number of events year round, from New Year's Eve, Halloween, and Christmas bashes, traditional Thanksgiving Dinner, local fundraisers, and more. The chef, Seth Levine, creates delectable ocean-fresh and local fare alongside a panoramic view of the ocean. Outdoor dining is an option during the warmer months. Open year round.

Buddhaberry

Has an incredibly variety of healthy frozen yogurt toppings from chia seeds and quinoa, to raw coconut and maca powder. My favorite frozen yogurt of theirs is the seasonal pumpkin, chai, and the salted caramel pretzel. Frozen yogurt is sold by the ounce. Look for their postcards inside that offer customers 10% off their order. Open seasonally.

The Buddhaberry

Montauk Juice Factory

Features locally produced treats, apparel, and of course their cold pressed juices. They offer seasonal juices and smoothies such as their Smashing Pumpkin Protein, and their Bonfire Cider. My favorite juices are their Beach Break (watermelon and mint), and the Liquid Sunshine (orange, pineapple, coconut water, lemon). Bottles come in 8oz and 16oz. Open year round.

Rick's Crabby Cowboy Cafe and Marina

This is a favorite waterfront spot for fresh seafood and delicious BBQ. Best selling menu items include Rick's pulled pork and ribs plate with their famous onion rings that are out of this world. Additional menu items include local, fresh fish, clams, Montauk Pearl Oysters from the on-site oyster farm, and lobster rolls. For the kids, which is also my favorite aspect of this restaurant, is the nightly s'mores by the fire pits, and a large lawn for kids to play on. This restaurant is open seasonally and serves lunch and dinner.

Joni's Kitchen Montauk

This is the perfect place for grab-and-go snacks, smoothies, juices, salads, and more for the beach and or a hiking trip. I love her Mucho Maca Smoothie and cookies. Please see my review for more information at: http://eastendtaste.com/jonis-kitchen-montauk/

LUNCH or The Lobster Roll

Located on the Napeague stretch, this is a very famous and absolutely delicious eatery featuring their famous lobster rolls. I prefer to order the lobster roll slider with their clam chowder. Don't pass up on desserts, they are so yummy here, especially the cupcakes! Happy Hour Margarita specials are popular in the late afternoons. I recommend visiting here on an off time to avoid the crowds, between 2 and 4pm.

The famous lobster roll that comes with a side of coleslaw

Restaurant reviews can be found at 27east.com and local insights at eastendtaste.com.

For making reservations during the summer, make them five days to a week in advance. For parties of six or more, I recommend a week to two weeks.

Make your reservations on OpenTable.com to get points toward a future gift card. OpenTable features many excellent restaurants in the Hamptons.

Climate

Summer temperatures average in the upper 70's by day, going down to the high 60's to low 70's at night. Always bring a sweatshirt and/or a jacket. I also recommend bringing a windbreaker for windy and/or rainy days. Water temperatures average in the 70's in the summer. Fall temperatures tend to linger in November because of the ocean's moderating effect. Winter temperatures average in the mid to upper 30's. There is snow usually from December through February, with an average of about one to two inches per snowfall.

Hotels

The hotels I recommend in Montauk include Gurney's Inn Resort and Spa (open all year), the Harborside (open March-December), Sole East (open May-October), Royal Atlantic Beach Resort (open all year), and the Ocean Surf Resort (open April-October). Many hotels are only opened seasonally. Check their websites for availability and additional information.

*Rates also increase significantly during Memorial Day and Labor Day weekend.

Money - ATMs, credit cards & the currency

Chase Bank is located in the heart of Montauk's village at 731 Old Montauk Highway. The three additional banks in the area are *Suffolk County National Bank, Capital One Bank,* and *Bridgehampton National Bank*.

Getting into Montauk

Via rail (LIRR), bus, or private vehicle driving on Montauk Highway/Old Montauk Highway. The 10C bus is the local Suffolk County transit bus that picks up in East Hampton and runs from there to Montauk a few times each day. The bus stops in the Village at the Hampton Jitney stop on S. Euclid Street. These are great, very inexpensive buses to take to from one town to the next. However, never expect the buses to be on time during the summer months.

Nightlife

Montauk is considered to have some of the best nightlife on the east end. More bars and restaurants are open late and feature live music, karaoke, and more. Here is a selection of my favorite nightlife spots:

- **Zum Schneider:** live music on the weekends, with celebrations for Oktoberfest, and other events throughout the year.

- **Sole East Resort and Restaurant:** features "Acoustic Sunsets" which begin July 4th weekend, and the Sole East Resort features DJ's around the pool on Saturdays and Sundays, and live music nightly at their restaurant. My favorite is their Brazilian Brunch on Sundays, with live Bossa Nova music.
- **Navy Beach:** music and events throughout the season, including the Navy SEAL Foundation benefit cocktail party in June.
- **Swallow East:** live music with different groups five nights a week, and Reggae Sundays, starting at 6pm.

Additional websites for information

Helpful websites for calendar information include:

- https://www.27east.com
- https://www.danspapers.com
- https://www.hamptons-magazine.com

Random tips

- Visit the **Farmer's Market** during the late spring, summer, and early autumn, which is every Thursday on the Village Green, from 9am-2pm.
- There are many **craft fairs** during the summer on the weekends. You can get some great deals on local artisan's photographs, jewelry, paintings, and more. Find the craft shows in the center of the Montauk Village at the circle or "The Plaza."

- The FITiST Collective, a one-stop place for an eclectic mix of fitness studios, offers many fitness classes across Montauk in July and August before Labor Day. Some of these classes are FREE and are sponsored by the fitness studios that are apart of the Collective. You can usually find more information on their website and/or their social media pages. Some of the fitness classes are held at the Montauk Beach House, a hotel that is popular with the 20-something crowd. Also at the Montauk Beach House (MBH) is fun, upbeat weekend and afternoon music spun by talented DJs, and a braid bar that pops up occasionally on the weekends.

(Montauk Beach House)

About the Author

Vanessa Gordon

Vanessa is a novelist, fitness instructor, English language instructor, and travel and specialty food writer. She earned her Master of Arts degree in Education from New York University and studied Literacy and British Literature at the University of Oxford. In her free time she enjoys reading antiquarian cookbooks, sunset paddle boarding, playing the violin, traveling, barre, t'ai chi, indoor cycling, essential oils, and volunteering at her local animal shelter. She lives in the Hamptons with her husband, daughter, and their cat, Abby.

Twitter: @EastEndTaste

Blog: www.eastendtaste.com

Unanchor
Chief Itinerary Coordinator

All maps are copyright OpenStreetMap contributors.
Please visit www.openstreetmap.org/copyright for more information.

Unanchor wants your opinion!

Your next travel adventure starts now. A simple review on Amazon will grant you and a travel buddy, friend, or human of your choosing any of the wonderful Unanchor digital itineraries for free.

What a deal!

Leave a Review

- Leave a review: http://www.amazon.com/unanchor

Collect your guides

- Send an email to reviews@unanchor.com with a link to your review.
- Wait with bated breath.
- Receive your new travel adventure in your inbox!

Other Unanchor Itineraries

Africa

- One Day in Africa - A Guide to Tangier
- Cape Town - What not to miss on a 4-day first-timers' itinerary
- Johannesburg/Pretoria: A 4-Day South Africa Tour Itinerary

Asia

- 4 Days in Bishkek On a Budget
- Beijing Must Sees, Must Dos, Must Eats - 3-Day Tour Itinerary
- 2 Days in Shanghai: A Budget-Conscious Peek at Modern China
- A 3-Day Tryst with 300-Year-Old Kolkata
- Kolkata (Calcutta): 2 Days of Highlights
- 3-Day Budget Delhi Itinerary
- Delhi in 3 Days - A Journey Through Time
- 3 Days Highlights of Mumbai
- Nozawa Onsen's Winter Secrets - A 3-Day Tour
- 3-Day Highlights of Tokyo
- Tour Narita During an Airport Layover
- 3 Days in the Vibrant City of Seoul and the Serene Countryside of Gapyeong
- A First Timer's Weekend Guide to Ulaanbaatar
- The Very Best of Moscow in 3 Days
- Saint Petersburg in Three Days

Central America and the Caribbean

- Old San Juan, Puerto Rico 2-Day Walking Itinerary
- Two Exciting Days in Dutch Sint Maarten - Hello Cruisers!
- Two Amazing Days in St. Croix, USVI - Hello Cruisers!

Europe

- Beginner's Iceland - A four-day self-drive itinerary
- Mostar - A City with Soul in 1 Day
- 3 Days in Brussels - The grand sites via the path less trodden
- Zagreb For Art Lovers: A Three-Day Itinerary
- 3-Day Prague Beer Pilgrimage
- Best of Prague - 3-Day Itinerary
- 3 Days in Copenhagen - Explore Like a Local
- Best of Copenhagen 2-Day Walking Itinerary
- Christmas in Copenhagen - A 2-Day Guide
- 3 Days in Helsinki
- Highlights of Budapest in 3 Days
- 3 Days in Dublin City - City Highlights, While Eating & Drinking Like a Local
- Weekend Break: Tbilisi - Crown Jewel of the Caucasus
- 2 Days In Berlin On A Budget
- A 3-Day Guide to Berlin, Germany
- 3 Days of Fresh Air in Moldova's Countryside
- Amsterdam 3-Day Alternative Tour: Not just the Red Light District
- Amsterdam Made Easy: A 3-Day Guide
- Two-day tour of Utrecht: the smaller, less touristy Amsterdam!
- Krakow: Three-Day Tour of Poland's Cultural Capital
- Best of Warsaw 2-Day Itinerary
- Lisbon in 3 Days: Budget Itinerary
- Braşov - Feel the Pulse of Transylvania in 3 Days
- Lausanne 1-Day Tour Itinerary
- Belgrade: 7 Days of History on Foot

France

- Paris to Chartres Cathedral: 1-Day Tour Itinerary
- A 3-Day Tour of Mont St Michel, Normandy and Brittany
- Art Lovers' Paris: A 2-Day Artistic Tour of the City of Lights
- Paris 1-Day Itinerary - Streets of Montmartre
- Paris 3-Day Walking Tour: See Paris Like a Local
- Paris 4-Day Winter Wonderland
- Paris for Free: 3 Days
- The Best of Paris in One Day

Greece
- Athens 3-Day Highlights Tour Itinerary
- Chania & Sfakia, Greece & Great Day Trips Nearby (5-Day Itinerary)
- Santorini, Greece in 3 Days: Living like a Local
- 2-Day Beach Tour: Travel like a Local in Sithonia Peninsula, Halkidiki, Greece
- Day Trip From Thessaloniki to Kassandra Peninsula, Halkidiki, Greece
- Thessaloniki, Greece - 3-Day Highlights Itinerary

Italy
- A Day on Lake Como, Italy
- 3-Day Florence Walking Tours
- Florence, Italy 3-Day Art & Culture Itinerary
- Milan Unknown - A 3-day tour itinerary
- 3 Days of Roman Adventure: spending time and money efficiently in Rome
- A 3-Day Tour Around Ancient Rome
- Discover Rome's Layers: A 3-Day Walking Tour
- See Siena in a Day
- Landscape, Food, & Trulli: 1 Week in Puglia, the Valle d'Itria, and Matera
- Three Romantic Walks in Venice

Spain
- 3-Day Highlights of Barcelona Itinerary
- FC Barcelona: More than a Club (A 1-Day Experience)
- Ibiza on a Budget - Three-Day Itinerary
- Three days exploring Logroño and La Rioja by public transport
- Málaga, Spain – 2-Day Tour from the Moors to Picasso
- Mijas - One Day Tour of an Andalucían White Village
- Two-Day Tour in Sunny Seville, Spain
- Best of Valencia 2-Day Guide

United Kingdom
- Bath: An Exploring Guide - 2-Day Itinerary
- History, Culture, and Craic: 3 Days in Belfast, Ireland
- 2-Day Brighton Best-of Walks & Activities
- Bristol in 2 Days: A Local's Guide
- Two-Day Self-Guided Walks - Cardiff

- The Best of Edinburgh: A 3-Day Journey from Tourist to Local
- 3-Day London Tour for Olympic Visitors
- An Insider's Guide to the Best of London in 3 Days
- Done London? A 3-day itinerary for off the beaten track North Norfolk
- London 1-Day Literary Highlights
- London for Free :: Three-Day Tour
- London's Historic City Wall Walk (1-2 days)
- London's South Bank - Off the Beaten Track 1-Day Tour
- London's Villages - A 3-day itinerary exploring Hampstead, Marylebone and Notting Hill
- Low-Cost, Luxury London - 3-Day Itinerary
- The 007 James Bond Day Tour of London
- MADchester - A Local's 3-Day Guide To Manchester
- One Day in Margate, UK on a Budget

Middle East

- Paphos 3-Day Itinerary: Live like a local!
- Adventure Around Amman: A 2-Day Itinerary
- Amman 2-Day Cultural Tour
- Doha 2-Day Stopover Cultural Tour
- Doha Surf and Turf: A two-day itinerary
- 3 Days as an Istanbulite: An Istanbul Itinerary
- Between the East and the West, a 3-Day Istanbul Itinerary

North America

Canada

- Relax in Halifax for Two Days Like a Local
- An Insider's Guide to Toronto: Explore the City Less Traveled in Three Days
- The Best of Toronto - 2-Day Itinerary
- Toronto: A Multicultural Retreat (3-day itinerary)

Mexico

- Cancun and Mayan Riviera 5-Day Itinerary (3rd Edition)
- Everything to see or do in Mexico City - 7-Day Itinerary
- Mexico City 3-Day Highlights Itinerary
- Todo lo que hay que ver o hacer en la Ciudad de México - Itinerario de 7 Días
- Your Chiapas Adventure: San Cristobal de las Casas and Palenque, Mexico 5-Day Itinerary

United States

East Coast

- Girls' 3-Day Weekend Summer Getaway in Asheville, NC
- Atlanta 3-Day Highlights
- Baltimore: A Harbor, Parks, History, Seafood & Art - 3-Day Itinerary
- Boston 2-Day Historic Highlights Itinerary
- Navigating Centuries of Boston's Nautical History in One Day
- Rainy Day Boston One-Day Itinerary
- Brooklyn, NY 2-Day Foodie Tour
- The Weekenders Guide To Burlington, Vermont
- A Local's Guide to the Hamptons 3 Day Itinerary
- Weekend Day Trip from New York City: The Wine & Whiskey Trail
- 2 Days Exploring Haunted Key West
- 3 Day PA Dutch Country Highlights (Lancaster County, PA)
- Day Trek Along the Hudson River
- A Local's Guide to Montauk, New York in 2 Days - From the Ocean to the Hills
- New Haven Highlights: Art, Culture & History 3-Day Itinerary
- Day Trip from New York City: Mountains, Falls, & a Funky Town
- 3-Day Amazing Asian Food Tour of New York City!
- Hidden Bars of New York City's East Village & Lower East Side: A 2-Evening Itinerary
- Jewish New York in Two Days
- Lower Key, Lower Cost: Lower Manhattan - 1-Day Itinerary
- New York City - First Timer's 2-Day Walking Tour
- New York City's Lower East Side, 1-Day Tour Itinerary
- New York Like A Native: Five Boroughs in Six Days
- 3-Day Discover Orlando Itinerary

- Five Days in the Wild Outer Banks of North Carolina
- Two Days in Philadelphia
- Pittsburgh: Three Days Off the Beaten Path
- Day Trip from New York City: Heights of the Hudson Valley (Bridges and Ridges)
- RVA Haunts, History, and Hospitality: Three Days in Richmond, Virginia
- Savannah 3-Day Highlights Itinerary
- Three Days in the Sunshine City of St. Petersburg, Florida
- Washington, DC in 4 Days
- Washington, DC: 3 Days Like a Local

Central US

- A Laid-Back Long Weekend in Austin, TX
- 3-Day Chicago Highlights Itinerary
- 6-Hour "Layover" Chicago
- Chicago Food, Art and Funky Neighborhoods in 3 Days
- Famous Art & Outstanding Restaurants in Chicago 1-Day Itinerary
- Family Weekend in Columbus, OH
- Ohio State Game Day Weekend
- Corpus Christi: The Insider Guide for a 4-Day Tour
- The Best of Kansas City: 3-Day Itinerary
- La Grange, Kentucky: A 3-Day Tour Itinerary
- Louisville: Three Days in Derby City
- New Orleans 3-Day Itinerary
- Paris Foodie Classics: 1 Day of French Food
- Wichita From Cowtown to Air Capital in 2 Days

West Coast

- Orange County 3-Day Budget Itinerary
- Cruisin' Asbury like a Local in 1 Day
- A Day on Bainbridge Island
- Beverly Hills, Los Angeles - 1-Day Tour
- Beer Lovers 3-Day Guide To Northern California
- The Best of Boulder, CO: A Three-Day Guide
- Lesser-known Oahu in 4 Days on a Budget
- Local's Guide to Oahu - 3-Day Tour Itinerary
- Summer in Jackson Hole: Local Tips for the Perfect Three to Five Day Adventure
- Tackling 10 Must-Dos on the Big Island in 3 Days
- Las Vegas - Gaming Destination Diversions - Ultimate 3-Day Itinerary

- Las Vegas on a Budget - 3-Day Itinerary
- 2-Day Los Angeles Vegan and Vegetarian Foodie Itinerary
- Downtown Los Angeles 1-Day Walking Tour
- Hollywood, Los Angeles - 1-Day Walking Tour
- Los Angeles 4-Day Itinerary (partly using Red Tour Bus)
- Los Angeles Highlights 3-Day Itinerary
- Los Angeles On A Budget - 4-Day Tour Itinerary
- Sunset Strip, Los Angeles - 1-Day Walking Tour
- An Active 2-3 Days In Moab, Utah
- Beyond the Vine: 2-Day Napa Tour
- Wine, Food, and Fun: 3 Days in Napa Valley
- Palm Springs, Joshua Tree & Salton Sea: A 3-Day Itinerary
- Portland Bike and Bite: A 2-Day Itinerary
- Three Days Livin' as a True and Local Portlander
- Weekend Tour of Portland's Craft Breweries, Wineries, & Distilleries
- Best of the Best: Three-Day San Diego Itinerary
- San Francisco 2-Day Highlights Itinerary
- San Francisco Foodie Weekend Itinerary
- The Tech Lover's 48-Hour Travel Guide to Silicon Valley & San Francisco
- Alaska Starts Here - 3 Days in Seward
- Three Days in Central California's Wine Country
- Tucson: 3 Days at the Intersection of Mexico, Native America & the Old West

Oceania

- The Blue Mountains: A weekend of nature, culture and history.
- A Weekend Snapshot of Melbourne
- An Afternoon & Evening in Melbourne's Best Hidden Bars
- Laneway Melbourne: A One-Day Walking Tour
- Magic of Melbourne 3-Day Tour
- Two Wheels and Pair of Cozzies: the Best of Newcastle in 3 Days
- Best of Perth's Most Beautiful Sights in 3 Days
- A Weekend Snapshot of Sydney
- Sydney, Australia - 3-Day **Best Of** Itinerary
- Enjoy the Rebuild - Christchurch 2-Day Tour
- The Best of Wellington: 3-Day Itinerary

South America

- An Insider's Guide to the Best of Buenos Aires in 3 Days
- Buenos Aires Best Kept Secrets: 2-Day Itinerary
- Sights & Sounds of São Paulo - 3-Day Itinerary
- Cuenca, Ecuador - A 3-Day Discovery Tour
- A 1-Day Foodie's Dream Tour of Arequipa
- Arequipa - A 2-Day Itinerary for First-Time Visitors
- Cusco and the Sacred Valley - a five-day itinerary for a first-time visitor
- Little Known Lima 3-Day Tour

Southeast Asia

- Between the Skyscrapers - Hong Kong 3-Day Discovery Tour
- Art and Culture in Ubud, Bali – 1-Day Highlights
- Go with the Sun to Borobudur & Prambanan in 1 Day
- A 3-Day Thrilla in Manila then Flee to the Sea
- Manila on a Budget: 2-Day Itinerary
- A First Timer's Guide to 3 Days in the City that Barely Sleeps - Singapore
- Family Friendly Singapore - 3 Days in the Lion City
- Singapore: 3 Fun-Filled Days on this Tiny Island
- The Affordable Side of Singapore: A 4-Day Itinerary
- The Two Worlds of Kaohsiung in 5 Days
- 72 Hours in Taipei: The All-rounder
- Girls' Weekend in Bangkok: Shop, Spa, Savour, Swoon
- The Ins and Outs of Bangkok: A 3-Day Guide
- Saigon 3-Day Beyond the Guidebook Itinerary

Unanchor is a global family for travellers to experience the world with the heart of a local.

Made in the USA
Columbia, SC
11 June 2019